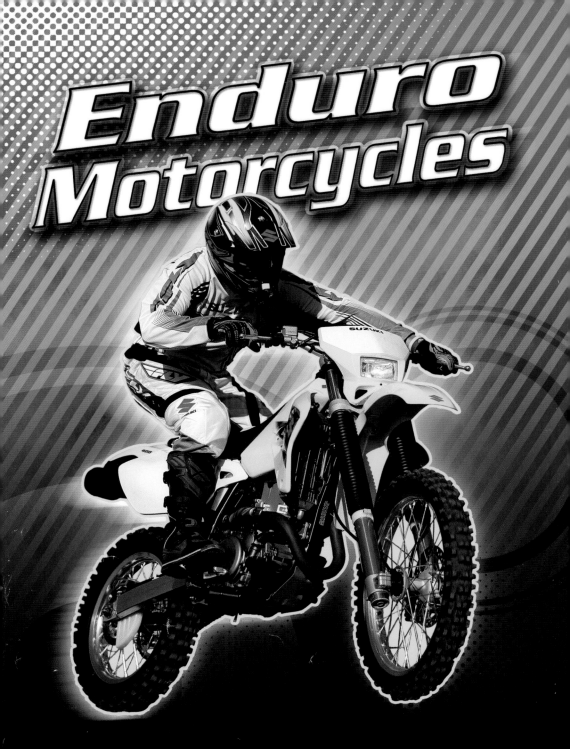

Enduro
Motorcycles

BY **JACK DAVID**

BELLWETHER MEDIA • MINNEAPOLIS, MN

™

Are you ready to take it to the extreme?
Torque books thrust you into the action-packed
world of sports, vehicles, and adventure. These books
may include dirt, smoke, fire, and dangerous stunts.
WARNING: read at your own risk.

Library of Congress Cataloging-in-Publication Data

David, Jack, 1968-
  Enduro motorcycles / by Jack David.
      p. cm. -- (Torque. Motorcycles)
  Includes bibliographical references and index.
  ISBN-13: 978-1-60014-133-1 (hbk. : alk. paper)
  ISBN-10: 1-60014-133-1 (hbk. : alk. paper)
  1. Trail bikes--Juvenile literature. 2. Motorcycles, Racing--Juvenile literature. 3. Moto-
cross--Juvenile literature. I. Title.

  TL441.D37 2008
  629.227'5--dc22

                                                                           2007014197

This edition first published in 2008 by Bellwether Media.

No part of this publication may be reproduced in whole or in part without written permission of
the publisher. For information regarding permission, write to Bellwether Media Inc., Attention:
Permissions Department, Post Office Box 1C, Minnetonka, MN 55345-9998.

CONTENTS

ENDURO MOTORCYCLES IN ACTION

The roar of an enduro motorcycle's engine fills the air. The tires rise and fall as they travel over dirt, rock, and tree roots. The rider slows down to steer around a sharp turn. Branches from a nearby tree whack the side of the bike as the rider turns.

FAST FACT
WORLD CHAMPIONSHIP ENDURO COURSES MUST BE AT LEAST 125 MILES (200 KILOMETERS) LONG. NO MORE THAN 30 PERCENT OF THIS DISTANCE CAN BE PAVED.

The rider sees a **checkpoint** at the top of a hill. Dirt kicks out from under the rear wheel as the motorcycle speeds up a hill. The rider crosses the checkpoint and notes his time.

He knows an enduro event is not like a normal race. Setting a top speed is not the goal. His goal is to cross checkpoints at set times. Enduro racing requires riders to keep a steady pace over a long and varied course.

WHAT IS AN ENDURO MOTORCYCLE?

Enduro motorcycles are dirt bikes built for this unique kind of event. Most of an enduro course is off-road. Enduro bikes handle well on dirt, rocks, gravel, and mud.

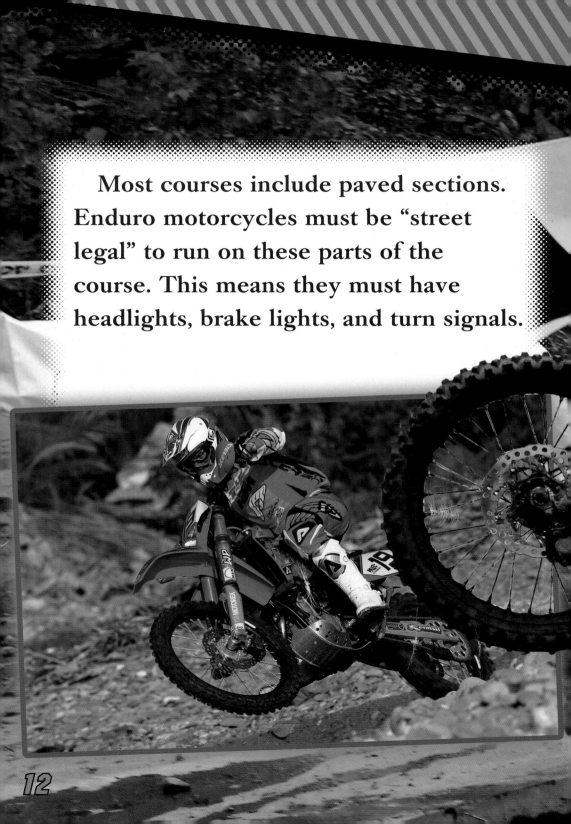

Most courses include paved sections. Enduro motorcycles must be "street legal" to run on these parts of the course. This means they must have headlights, brake lights, and turn signals.

13

FEATURES

Enduro motorcycles have all the features of a dirt bike. They have "knobby" tires with deep **tread**. The bumps and grooves of the tread give enduros a good grip on loose surfaces. They also have strong **suspension systems** to absorb the bumps and jolts of rough **terrain**.

FAST FACT
MANY ENDURO RIDERS USE ROLL CHARTS. THESE SMALL PIECES OF PAPER LIST THE RACE'S MAJOR TURNS AND KNOWN CHECKPOINTS.

Other features help riders on the course. Small engines keep enduros light and easy to handle. Narrow handlebars help riders easily slip past tree branches and other obstacles. **Skid plates** protect the bottom of the bike from mud, rocks, and logs. Most enduro motorcycles also have a computer to help the rider track time and distance.

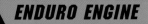

ENDURO ENGINE

17

THE ENDURO MOTORCYCLE EXPERIENCE

Enduro events are long and difficult. Many last three or four hours. Long races over rough terrain require both a rider and a motorcycle with great **endurance**. The clock means everything to an enduro rider. Riders are timed at every checkpoint. Reaching a checkpoint too early or too late costs a rider points.

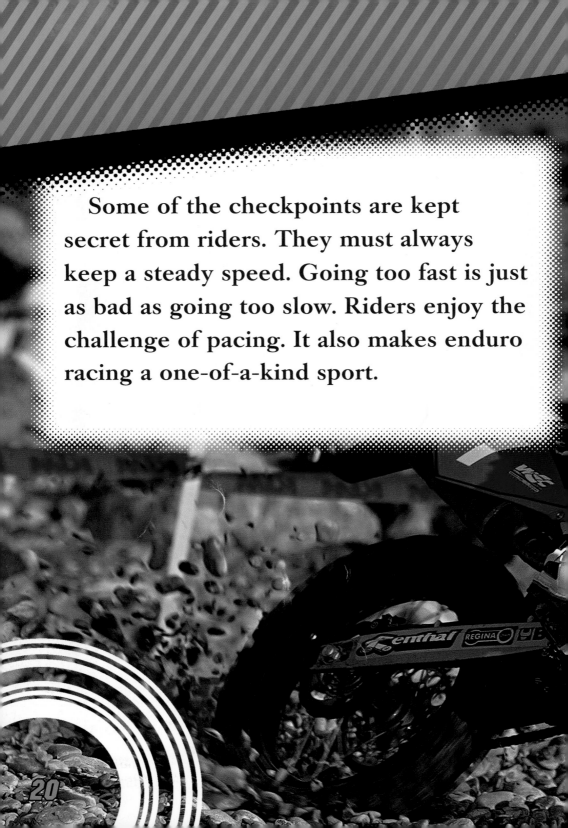

Some of the checkpoints are kept secret from riders. They must always keep a steady speed. Going too fast is just as bad as going too slow. Riders enjoy the challenge of pacing. It also makes enduro racing a one-of-a-kind sport.

FAST FACT

FINLAND'S JUHA SALMINEN IS ONE OF THE WORLD'S MOST FAMOUS ENDURO RIDERS. HE WON FIVE STRAIGHT OVERALL WORLD ENDURO CHAMPIONSHIPS FROM 2000 TO 2004.

GLOSSARY

checkpoint–one of many stations along an enduro course at which riders are scored

endurance–having the ability to perform an activity for a long period of time

skid plate–a steel plate affixed to the underside of a dirt bike to protect the bike from loose rocks, dirt, and other debris

suspension system–a series of springs and shock absorbers that connect the body of a vehicle to its wheels

terrain–the natural surface features of the land

tread–the series of bumps and grooves on a tire that help it grip rough surfaces

TO LEARN MORE

AT THE LIBRARY

Healy, Nick. *Enduro Racing*. Mankato, Minn.: Capstone Press, 2006.

Hill, Lee Sullivan. *Motorcycles*. Minneapolis, Minn.: Lerner Publications Co., 2004.

ON THE WEB

Learning more about motorcycles is as easy as 1, 2, 3.

1. Go to www.factsurfer.com

2. Enter "motorcycles" into search box.

3. Click the "Surf" button and you will see a list of related web sites.

With factsurfer.com, finding more information is just a click away.

INDEX